Tennyson

A dreamer and a poet.

Mrs H

A smile and a snack for everyone.

Twigs

Ready to learn and play every day.

CWR, Waverley Abbey House, Waverley Lane, Farnham, Surrey GU9 8EP

National Distributors

UK (and countries not listed below): CWR, PO Box 230, Farnham, Surrey GU9 8XG. Tel: (01252) 784710   Outside UK (44) 1252 784710

AUSTRALIA: CMC Australasia, PO Box 519, Belmont, Victoria 3216. Tel: (03) 5241 3288

CANADA: CMC Distribution Ltd, PO Box 7000, Niagara on the Lake, Ontario L0S 1J0. Tel: (0800) 325 1297

GHANA: Challenge Enterprises of Ghana, PO Box 5723, Accra. Tel: (021) 222437/223249   Fax: (021) 226227

HONG KONG: Cross Communications Ltd, 1/F, 562A Nathan Road, Kowloon. Tel: 2780 1188 Fax: 2770 6229

INDIA: Crystal Communications, 10-3-18/4/1, East Marredpally, Secunderabad – 500 026. Tel/Fax: (040) 7732801

KENYA: Keswick Bookshop, PO Box 10242, Nairobi. Tel: (02) 331692/226047

MALAYSIA: Salvation Book Centre (M) Sdn Bhd, 23 Jalan SS 2/64, 47300 Petaling Jaya, Selangor.
Tel: (03) 78766411/78766797 Fax: (03) 78757066/78756360

NEW ZEALAND: CMC New Zealand Ltd, Private Bag, 17910 Green Lane, Auckland. Tel: (09) 5249393 Fax: (09) 5222137

NIGERIA: FBFM, Helen Baugh House, 96 St Finbarr's College Road, Akoka, Lagos. Tel: (01) 7747429/4700218/825775/827264

PHILIPPINES: OMF Literature Inc, 776 Boni Avenue, Mandaluyong City. Tel: (02) 531 2183 Fax: (02) 531 1960

REPUBLIC OF IRELAND: Scripture Union, 40 Talbot Street, Dublin 1. Tel: (01) 8363764

SINGAPORE: Campus Crusade Asia Ltd, 315 Outram Road, 06-08 Tan Boon Liat Building, Singapore 169074. Tel: (065) 222 3640

SOUTH AFRICA: Struik Christian Books, 80 MacKenzie Street, PO Box 1144, Cape Town 8000. Tel: (021) 462 4360 Fax: (021) 461 3612

SRI LANKA: Christombu Books, 27 Hospital Street, Colombo 1. Tel: (01) 433142/328909

TANZANIA: CLC Christian Book Centre, PO Box 1384, Mkwepu Street, Dar es Salaam. Tel: (051) 2119439

UGANDA: New Day Bookshop, PO Box 2021, Kampala. Tel: (041) 255377

ZIMBABWE: Word of Life Books, Shop 4, Memorial Building, 35 S Machel Avenue, Harare. Tel: (04) 781305 Fax: (04) 774739

For e-mail addresses, visit the CWR web site: www.cwr.org.uk

Tails: Twigs and the Treasure Box

© 2001 Karyn Henley. All rights reserved. Exclusively administered by Child Sensitive Communication, LLC

Text and characterisations by Karyn Henley

Models created by: Debbie Smith

Photographed by: Roger Walker

Designer: Christine Reissland at CWR

Editor: Lynette Brooks

Illustrator: Sheila Anderson Hardy of Advocate

Printed in Spain by Espace Grafic Navarra

ISBN 1 85345 158 4

Published 2001 by CWR

Unless otherwise identified, all Scripture quotations in this publication are from the Holy Bible: International Children's Bible copyright © 1983, 1988, 1991 by Word Publishing.

Twigs and
the Treasure Box

"I will praise you, Lord, with all my heart."

Psalm 9:1

Karyn Henley

Twigs and the Treasure Box

Plip, plop, drip, drop. A slow rain tapped on the window pane. At the kitchen table, Twigs was hard at work. Snip and clip. Paper and glue. Buttons and beads. Twigs was making a small treasure chest out of an old box. When he had finished, he showed his mum.

"What a wonderful treasure box," said Mrs H. "It's just right for holding something very important."

"Yes," said Twigs. "I'm going to put something very important in my box."

By that time, the rain had stopped, and the sun was shining. So Twigs ran outdoors with his treasure chest. "Something very important," said Twigs, thinking hard. "What is something very important to put in my treasure box?"

Suddenly Twigs knew. Just that morning when he had complained about the rain, his mum had said the rain was very important. It made plants grow and gave us water to drink. So Twigs ran to Chester's tree. He stood underneath a low branch and opened his treasure box to catch a drop of rainwater falling from a leaf.

"What are you doing?" called Chester from his tree house.

"I'm trying to catch rainwater in my treasure box," said Twigs. "Rain is very important."

"That's true," said Chester. "But I think sunshine is more important than rain. When it rains, I have to stay indoors. But when the sun shines, I can go out and play!"

"You're right!" said Twigs. He hadn't thought of it that way. "Thanks!" Then he closed his treasure box. "Come on, Chester. Let's go and find some sunshine to catch."

Twigs and Chester ran until they came to a place where the sun shone brightly through the trees, making a sun puddle on the ground. There, Twigs opened his box and held it up in the sunlight.

Just then, Mimi walked by. "Hello you two," she said. "What are you doing?"

"I'm putting sunshine in my treasure box," said Twigs. "Chester says that sunshine is very important."

"That's true," said Mimi. "But I think clouds are more important than the sun. Look, the sun is always the same: big and round and bright. But clouds are interesting shapes and different sizes. New clouds come into the sky every day. I love to draw clouds."

"Mmm, you're right!" said Twigs. He had never thought of it that way. "Thanks" he said, closing his treasure box. "Let's go and find some clouds to catch!"

They all ran to Owlfred's tree. "Hello! Hello! Owlfred, are you home?" they called.

"Whoo-oo's there?" called Owlfred from inside his tree house.

"It's me," said Twigs.

"Whoo-oo's me?" asked Owlfred, looking down at Twigs. "Oh, you're me," said Owlfred when he saw him. "I mean you're you and I'm me. But you're the me who was calling to me. Oh, dear, dear me! I'm all muddled up here."

Owlfred ruffled his feathers and cleared his mind.

"I'm sorry. I'm in the middle of an experiment. Hello Chester. Hello Mimi. Why don't you all come on up and talk to me?"

"I was just wondering if you would do something special for me," said Twigs. "I will if I can and I can if I will," said Owlfred. "What is this something you want me to do?"

"I need you to fly up to the sky and bring me back a piece of cloud,"
said Twigs. "Just a small piece to put into my treasure box, because
Mimi says that clouds are very important."

"But you can't hold a piece of cloud in a box," said Owlfred. "Besides, I think the wind is much more important than clouds. The wind is powerful. It pushes the clouds across the sky. It lifts me up high when I fly. And I can do experiments with the wind!"

"You're right!" said Twigs. He had never thought of it that way. "Thanks Owlfred," he said, closing his treasure box. "Let's all go and find some wind to catch!"

Twigs, Mimi and Chester ran together out of the woods and into the meadow. Owlfred flew along too. They felt the wind blowing very gently.

Twigs opened his treasure box and held it out. The wind blew into it. Twigs looked inside the box.

"How will you know when you've got enough?" asked Chester.

"Enough what?" asked a voice.

They all turned to see Tennyson sitting by his rock, busily writing songs.

"Enough wind," said Twigs. "I'm catching the wind in my treasure box."

"So, my little friend is catching some wind," said Tennyson.

"Yes," said Twigs. "Owlfred says the wind is very important. But Mimi says the clouds are very important. Chester says the sunshine is very important. And Mum says the rain is very important."

"Different things are important to different people," said Tennyson. "But there's one thing that's important to all of us: Owlfred, Mimi, Chester, your Mum, and even me. It's the most important thing in the whole world."

"What is it?" asked Twigs.

"That's a very good question," said Tennyson. "It's a question that someone asked Jesus long ago."

"And what did Jesus say?" asked Twigs.

Tennyson closed his eyes and smiled. "Jesus said that the most important thing is to 'love the Lord your God with all your heart, all your soul, all your mind, and all your strength.'"

"Wow!" said Twigs. "So that's the most important thing. But how do I show God I love him?"

"You worship him," said Tennyson.

"Worship? What does that mean? How do I do that?" asked Twigs.

"Well," said Chester. "How do you show your mum you love her?"

"I give her a kiss and a hug. And I tell her I love her," said Twigs.

"You can do the same with God," said Tennyson. "Talk to him. Sing to him. Tell him you love him. Show him that he's the most important of all."

"But I can't see God," said Twigs.

"You can't see the wind either," said Owlfred. "But you can see what it does. You can't see God. But you can see what he does."

Twigs looked. The wind was blowing the grasses and flowers. They seemed to be nodding at Twigs.

Suddenly Twigs had an idea. "I know what I'll put in my treasure box!" he said. He ran back through the woods, all the way home.

Snip and clip. Cut and colour. Twigs made a paper heart. He wrote on the heart, "I love you, God." He put the heart in his treasure box.

Then Twigs opened his arms wide and said, "Here's a kiss and hug for you, God."

Twigs closed his eyes and smiled. He couldn't see God, but he could feel God hugging him back.

"I will praise you, Lord, with all my heart"

Psalm 9:1